The Psychology of Eating:
How Your Mind Influences Your Food Choices

By

Tommy Blair

Table of Contents

- The effects of dieting and weight loss on the body's hunger and satiety signals

Chapter 2
Emotions and Eating

- The relationship between mood and food cravings
- Emotional eating and its impact on health and well-being
- Strategies for managing emotional eating and developing healthier coping mechanisms

Chapter 3
Cognitive Factors in Eating

- The role of beliefs, attitudes, and expectations in food preferences

- The influence of cognitive biases and heuristics on food choices
- Cognitive-behavioral techniques for improving eating habits and promoting healthy behaviors

Chapter 4
Social and Environmental Influences on Eating

- The impact of social norms and peer pressure on eating behavior
- The role of food availability, accessibility, and convenience in shaping our choices
- Strategies for navigating social and environmental factors to make healthier food choices

Chapter 5

Eating Disorders and Disordered Eating

- An overview of the diagnostic criteria for eating disorders
- The prevalence and consequences of disordered eating behaviors
- Evidence-based treatments for eating disorders and related conditions

Chapter 6
Mindful Eating and Intuitive Eating

- The principles and benefits of mindful and intuitive eating
- Techniques for cultivating mindfulness and intuition in eating
- The role of mindfulness and intuition in promoting

Introduction

The Mind-Body Connection in Eating

The way we eat is influenced by a complex interplay of biological, psychological, and social factors. Our choices around food are not only driven by physical hunger and nutritional needs but also by emotions, beliefs, and cultural norms. This book explores the role of psychology in shaping our eating habits and how our minds influence our food choices.

Research has shown that our thoughts, feelings, and attitudes can impact our food preferences, portion sizes, and eating behaviors. For example, we may turn to comfort foods when we are stressed or seek out certain foods because we associate them with positive memories or experiences. Our cognitive biases and heuristics, such as the availability heuristic or the anchoring effect, can also affect how we perceive food and make decisions around it.

Furthermore, social and environmental factors play a significant role in our eating habits. We are influenced by the food choices of those around us, as well as by the availability and accessibility of different foods. The media and advertising also shape our attitudes towards food, with a focus on certain diets or food trends.

Mindfulness and self-awareness are essential in eating, allowing us to become more attuned to our physical and emotional signals around food. By understanding the psychology of eating, we can make more informed and intentional choices around what we eat, improving our overall health and well-being.

In this book, we will explore the biological, emotional, cognitive, social, and cultural factors that influence our eating habits. We will examine the impact of different eating patterns, including emotional eating, mindful eating, and intuitive eating, and explore evidence-based strategies for improving our relationship with food. By applying psychological principles to our eating habits, we can cultivate a healthier and more sustainable approach to nutrition.

The role of psychology in shaping our eating habits

Our eating habits are heavily influenced by psychology. Our food choices and eating behaviors are not only influenced by our physical hunger and nutritional needs but also by our thoughts, emotions, beliefs, and social and cultural contexts.

Research has shown that our thoughts and attitudes towards food can impact our food preferences and eating behaviors. For example, if we view healthy eating as a chore or restrictive, we may be less likely to choose healthy foods or stick to a balanced diet. On the other hand, if we view healthy eating as a positive and enjoyable aspect of self-care, we may be more motivated to make healthier choices.

Our emotions can also influence our eating habits. We may turn to comfort foods when we are feeling stressed, sad, or anxious, or use food as a way to cope with difficult emotions. Emotional eating can lead to overeating or unhealthy food choices, which can have negative impacts on our physical and mental health.

Cultural and social norms also shape our eating habits. We may be influenced by the food choices of those around us, such as our family, friends, and colleagues. Additionally, media and advertising can shape our attitudes towards food, with a focus on certain diets or food trends.

Psychology can also play a role in addressing disordered eating behaviors, such as binge eating disorder, anorexia nervosa, and bulimia nervosa. Cognitive-behavioral therapy (CBT) and other evidence-based treatments focus on identifying and addressing the underlying psychological factors that contribute to these disorders.

By understanding the role of psychology in shaping our eating habits, we can become more aware of our thoughts and emotions around food and make more informed and intentional choices around what we eat. This can help promote healthier eating habits and improve our overall physical and mental health.

The influence of culture, media, and advertising on our food choices

Culture, media, and advertising all play significant roles in influencing our food choices. These external factors shape our attitudes, perceptions, and behaviors related to food and can have a significant impact on our eating habits.

- **Cultural Influences**

Our cultural background, traditions, and social norms can greatly influence our food choices. Different cultures have their own unique food preferences, dietary patterns, and eating rituals. For example, some cultures may prioritize a plant-based diet, while others may emphasize meat and dairy consumption. Cultural celebrations, holidays, and family gatherings also often involve specific foods and meals that are culturally significant.

- **Media Influences**

The media, including television, magazines, social media, and food blogs, can shape our attitudes and perceptions about food. Media often promotes certain diets, food trends, and celebrity-endorsed eating patterns, influencing our food choices. Food advertising, in particular, can impact our preferences and perceptions about different foods, leading to increased consumption of less healthy foods that are heavily marketed.

- **Advertising Influences**

Advertising, both traditional and digital, plays a significant role in shaping our food choices. Food companies invest heavily in advertising to promote their products, using persuasive techniques and appealing visuals to influence our perceptions and preferences. Food packaging, labeling, and branding also impact our choices, as well as the placement of food products in grocery stores and other retail settings.

These cultural, media, and advertising influences can sometimes lead to unhealthy eating habits, such as the overconsumption of processed foods, sugary beverages, and fast foods. They can also contribute to the development of unrealistic body ideals, disordered eating patterns, and a distorted perception of what constitutes a healthy diet.

It is essential to be mindful of the influence of culture, media, and advertising on our food choices and to critically evaluate the information and messages we receive. Developing awareness of these external factors can help us make more informed and intentional food choices that align with our individual nutritional needs and overall health goals.

The importance of mindfulness and self-awareness in eating

Mindfulness and self-awareness play crucial roles in eating and can significantly impact our relationship with food. They involve being present and fully attentive to our thoughts, feelings, sensations, and behaviors related to eating, without judgment or distraction.

Here are some ways in which mindfulness and self-awareness are important in eating:

- **Sensory awareness**

Mindfulness allows us to fully engage our senses in the eating experience, including noticing the colors, textures, flavors, and aromas of our food. By being present and attentive to the sensory aspects of eating, we can enhance our enjoyment and satisfaction from food, leading to a more pleasurable eating experience.

- **Hunger and fullness cues**

Mindfulness helps us tune into our body's hunger and fullness cues, allowing us to eat in response to our physiological needs. By paying attention to our body's signals, we can avoid mindless eating, emotional eating, or overeating, and develop a healthier relationship with food.

- **Emotional awareness**

Mindfulness and self-awareness can help us become more attuned to our emotional state and how it may impact our eating habits. It can help us identify emotional triggers for eating, such as stress, boredom, or sadness, and develop healthier coping strategies instead of turning to food.

- **Thought patterns**

Mindfulness allows us to observe our thoughts and beliefs related to food without judgment. This can help us become aware of any negative or distorted thought patterns, such as rigid dieting rules or negative self-talk, that may impact our eating behaviors. By identifying and challenging these thoughts, we can develop a more positive and balanced mindset around food.

- **Eating behaviors**

Self-awareness helps us become more conscious of our eating behaviors, such as eating speed, portion sizes, and eating in response to external cues. By being mindful of our eating behaviors, we can make more intentional choices, develop healthier eating habits, and avoid mindless or automatic eating.

- **Food choices**

Mindfulness and self-awareness can also help us make more conscious and informed food choices. By being aware of our nutritional needs, food preferences, and the impact of food on our well-being, we can make choices that align with our individual health goals and values.

- **Body acceptance**

Mindfulness and self-awareness can promote body acceptance by helping us develop a non-judgmental and compassionate attitude towards our body. This can lead to a healthier body image and a more positive relationship with food, free from guilt, shame, or negative body-related thoughts.

Incorporating mindfulness and self-awareness into our eating habits can foster a healthier and more balanced approach to food. It allows us to be present, attuned, and intentional in our eating behaviors, leading to improved overall well-being and a positive relationship with food.

Chapter 1

The Biology of Appetite and Satiety

Appetite and satiety are regulated by a complex interplay of physiological mechanisms involving hormones, neurotransmitters, and other biological factors. Understanding the biology of appetite and satiety can provide insights into the physiological processes that influence our hunger and fullness cues, and can help inform strategies for managing eating behaviors and promoting healthy eating habits.

Here are some key aspects of the biology of appetite and satiety:

- **Hormonal regulation**

Hormones play a crucial role in regulating appetite and satiety. Ghrelin, known as the "hunger hormone," is produced in the stomach and stimulates appetite. Leptin, known as the "satiety hormone," is produced by adipose tissue (fat cells) and signals to the brain that we are full. Other hormones involved in appetite regulation include cholecystokinin (CCK), peptide YY (PYY), insulin, and glucagon-like peptide 1 (GLP-1). These hormones work together to send signals to the brain that regulate our hunger and fullness cues.

- **Neurotransmitter involvement**

Neurotransmitters are chemical messengers in the brain that play a role in appetite and satiety regulation. Serotonin, dopamine, and norepinephrine are neurotransmitters that are involved in regulating hunger, fullness, and mood. For example, serotonin is known to play a role in appetite suppression and mood regulation, while dopamine is associated with reward and motivation, which can impact eating behaviors.

- **Brain regions involved**

Several regions of the brain are involved in the regulation of appetite and satiety. The hypothalamus, a region located at the base of the brain, plays a central role in appetite regulation, receiving and integrating signals from various hormones and neurotransmitters. The amygdala, prefrontal cortex, and insula are also involved in the processing of emotions, reward, and decision-making related to food intake.

- **Energy balance and metabolism**

The body's energy balance, which is the balance between energy intake (from food) and energy expenditure (through physical activity and metabolism), also plays a role in appetite and satiety regulation. When we consume more energy than we expend, it can lead to weight gain and increased appetite. On the other hand, when we expend more energy than we consume, it can lead to weight loss and increased hunger signals.

- **Genetic and epigenetic factors**

Genetic and epigenetic factors, which are influenced by our genes and environmental factors, can also play a role in appetite and satiety regulation. Some individuals may have genetic predispositions that affect their hunger and fullness cues, metabolism, and response to different types of food, which can influence their eating behaviors and weight regulation.

Understanding the biological mechanisms that regulate appetite and satiety can help us make informed choices about our eating behaviors and develop strategies for managing hunger and fullness cues. It's important to note that appetite and satiety regulation are complex and multi-faceted, involving various physiological factors that interact with psychological, environmental, and social factors. A holistic approach that takes into account the interplay between biology, psychology, and the environment can be beneficial in promoting healthy eating habits and overall well-being. Consulting with qualified healthcare professionals, such as registered dietitians or healthcare providers, can provide personalized guidance and support in navigating the biology of appetite and satiety.

The physiological mechanisms that regulate hunger and fullness

The physiological mechanisms that regulate hunger and fullness are complex and involve a variety of factors, including hormones, neural pathways, and environmental cues.

Here are some of the main mechanisms involved:

- **Ghrelin**

Ghrelin is a hormone produced in the stomach that stimulates appetite. When the stomach is empty, ghrelin levels rise, sending a signal to the brain that it's time to eat.

- **Leptin**

Leptin is a hormone produced by fat cells that helps regulate appetite and energy balance. When fat stores are high, leptin levels rise, signaling to the brain that the body has enough energy and reducing appetite.

- **Insulin**

Insulin, a hormone secreted by the pancreas, helps to regulate blood sugar levels. It also plays a role in appetite regulation by suppressing the release of ghrelin and stimulating the release of leptin.

- **Peptide YY**

Peptide YY is a hormone produced in the small intestine in response to food intake. It signals to the brain that the body has received enough food and helps reduce appetite.

- **Neural pathways**

The brain plays a crucial role in regulating hunger and fullness. The hypothalamus, in particular, is an important center for appetite regulation, receiving signals from hormones, the gut, and other areas of the brain involved in processing taste and smell.

- **Environmental cues**

Environmental cues, such as the sight and smell of food, also play a role in appetite regulation. For example, the sight and smell of food can stimulate the release of ghrelin and increase appetite, even if the body doesn't need more food.

- **Gut-brain communication**

The gut and the brain communicate bidirectionally through a complex network of nerves, hormones, and signaling molecules. Signals from the gut, such as stretch receptors and nutrient-sensing cells, send messages to the brain about the state of the digestive system, influencing hunger and fullness cues.

Overall, the regulation of hunger and fullness is a complex process involving a variety of physiological mechanisms. Understanding these mechanisms can help us make healthier food choices and maintain a healthy weight.

The role of hormones, neurotransmitters, and other biological factors in eating behavior

Biological factors, including hormones and neurotransmitters, play a significant role in influencing eating behavior. These physiological factors interact with our brain and body to regulate our appetite, food preferences, and overall eating patterns.

Here are some of the key roles of hormones, neurotransmitters, and other biological factors in eating behavior:

- **Hormones**

Hormones are chemical messengers produced by various organs in our body that help regulate our appetite and food intake.

For example:

Ghrelin: As mentioned earlier, ghrelin is a hormone produced in the stomach that stimulates appetite and promotes food intake.

Leptin: Leptin is a hormone produced by fat cells that helps regulate appetite and energy balance. It sends signals to the brain to reduce appetite when fat stores are high.

Insulin: Insulin is a hormone produced by the pancreas that regulates blood sugar levels, but it also plays a role in appetite regulation by suppressing the release of ghrelin and stimulating the release of leptin.

Cholecystokinin (CCK): CCK is a hormone released in the small intestine in response to food intake. It signals to the brain to reduce appetite and promote feelings of fullness.

- **Neurotransmitters**

Neurotransmitters are chemical messengers in the brain that transmit signals between nerve cells and play a crucial role in regulating eating behavior.

For example:

Serotonin: Serotonin is a neurotransmitter that helps regulate mood, appetite, and satiety. Low serotonin levels have been associated with increased appetite and cravings for high-carbohydrate foods.

Dopamine: Dopamine is a neurotransmitter involved in reward and pleasure. It plays a role in food reward and motivation, influencing our food choices and eating behaviors.

- **Brain regions**

Various regions of the brain are involved in regulating eating behavior.

For example:

Hypothalamus: The hypothalamus is a key brain region involved in appetite regulation, energy balance, and satiety. It receives signals from hormones, neurotransmitters, and other areas of the brain to regulate eating behavior.

Prefrontal cortex: The prefrontal cortex is involved in decision-making, impulse control, and self-regulation, which play a role in food choices and eating behaviors.

- **Genetic and epigenetic factors**

Our genes and epigenetic factors can also influence eating behavior. Genetic and epigenetic variations can impact our metabolism, hormonal regulation, neurotransmitter function, and other physiological processes related to eating behavior, influencing our food preferences, eating patterns, and body weight regulation.

Understanding the role of hormones, neurotransmitters, and other biological factors in eating behavior provides insights into the physiological mechanisms that influence our food choices, appetite, and overall eating patterns. It highlights the complex interplay between our brain, body, and genetics in shaping our eating behaviors and can inform strategies for healthy eating and weight management.

The effects of dieting and weight loss on the body's hunger and satiety signals

Dieting and weight loss can have significant effects on the body's hunger and satiety signals. When we reduce our caloric intake through dieting or weight loss, it can trigger a series of physiological responses that impact our hunger and satiety cues.

Here are some of the effects of dieting and weight loss on the body's hunger and satiety signals:

- **Increased hunger**

When we eat fewer calories than our body needs for energy, it can result in a calorie deficit. In response to this deficit, the body may increase the production of hunger hormones, such as ghrelin, and decrease the production of satiety hormones, such as leptin. This can lead to increased hunger and cravings, making it challenging to stick to a reduced-calorie diet.

- **Altered satiety cues**

Dieting and weight loss can also impact our body's perception of fullness. Studies have shown that rapid weight loss or severe calorie restriction can disrupt the normal signaling of satiety hormones, such as cholecystokinin (CCK) and peptide YY (PYY), leading to reduced feelings of fullness even after eating a sufficient amount of food. This can result in overeating or a loss of satiety cues, which may affect weight management efforts.

- **Changes in taste preferences**

Dieting and weight loss can also impact our taste preferences. Research has shown that when we are in a state of caloric deficit, our taste preferences may shift towards higher calorie and sweeter foods, as the body seeks to compensate for the energy deficit. This can lead to increased cravings for high-calorie foods, making it harder to stick to a healthy eating plan.

- **Altered metabolism**

Dieting and weight loss can also affect our metabolism, which can impact hunger and satiety signals. When we eat fewer calories than our body needs, our metabolism may slow down in an attempt to conserve energy. This can reduce the production of satiety hormones and increase hunger, making it challenging to maintain weight loss.

- **Psychological factors**

In addition to physiological changes, psychological factors also play a role in the effects of dieting and weight loss on hunger and satiety signals. Dieting can lead to psychological stress, anxiety, and increased focus on food, which can impact our perception of hunger and satiety cues.

Understanding the effects of dieting and weight loss on the body's hunger and satiety signals can help us be mindful of the challenges and potential changes in appetite during weight management efforts. It highlights the importance of taking a holistic approach to weight management that includes considering both physiological and psychological factors to support long-term success.

Chapter 2

Emotions and Eating

Emotions can have a huge influence on our eating behavior. Many people turn to food as a way of coping with stress, anxiety, depression, boredom, or other emotional states. Emotional eating can lead to overeating or consuming unhealthy foods, which can negatively impact our physical and emotional well-being.

Here are some ways that emotions can affect eating behavior:

- **Stress eating**

Stress can trigger the release of cortisol, a hormone that can increase appetite and promote overeating. When we're stressed, we may turn to high-calorie, high-fat foods as a way of coping.

- **Boredom eating**

When we're bored, we may turn to food as a way of filling the time or finding pleasure. Overeating and mindless snacking can result from this.

- **Comfort eating**

Many people turn to food as a way of comforting themselves when they're feeling sad or lonely. Comfort foods are often high in calories and can contribute to weight gain.

- **Emotional suppression**

Some people may use food to suppress or numb emotions that they find difficult to deal with. This can result in binge eating or overeating.

- **Body image issues**

Negative emotions such as shame, guilt, or low self-esteem can impact our relationship with food and our body image. This can lead to restrictive eating, disordered eating, or compulsive overeating.

To manage emotional eating, it's important to develop healthy coping strategies that don't involve food. This can include exercise, meditation, deep breathing, or talking to a therapist or support group.

Practicing mindful eating, where you pay attention to your hunger and fullness cues, can also help you become more aware of your emotional triggers and develop a healthier relationship with food.

The relationship between mood and food cravings

The relationship between mood and food cravings is complex and can vary from person to person. While emotions can influence our food cravings, food can also affect our mood through various physiological and psychological mechanisms.

Here are some key points to understand the relationship between mood and food cravings:

- **Emotional triggers**

Certain emotions, such as stress, sadness, or anxiety, can trigger food cravings, particularly for high-calorie, high-sugar, or high-fat foods. This may be due to the brain's response to stress, which can lead to increased cravings for comfort foods as a way of coping with negative emotions.

- **Neurotransmitters and hormones**

Our mood is closely linked to neurotransmitters and hormones in the brain, such as serotonin, dopamine, and endorphins, which play a role in regulating mood, pleasure, and reward. Some foods, particularly those high in sugar and fat, can temporarily boost these neurotransmitters, leading to temporary mood improvement and reinforcing the craving for these types of foods.

- **Psychological factors**

Our thoughts, beliefs, and attitudes towards food can also influence our food cravings. For example, associating certain foods with positive emotions or memories can trigger cravings for those foods when we're in a certain mood or emotional state.

- **Habitual patterns**

Over time, we may develop habitual patterns of using food as a way to cope with emotions or to reward ourselves. For example, reaching for a pint of ice cream after a stressful day at work may become a habitual response to stress, leading to cravings for ice cream whenever we feel stressed.

- **Nutritional deficiencies**

Certain nutrient deficiencies, such as low levels of serotonin precursor tryptophan or magnesium, can impact mood and lead to food cravings. In some cases, cravings for specific foods may be the body's way of signaling a need for certain nutrients.

- **Cultural and societal influences**

Cultural and societal factors can also impact our food cravings. For example, food advertisements, social norms, and cultural traditions can shape our preferences and cravings for certain foods, even when we're not in a specific emotional state.

Understanding the relationship between mood and food cravings can help us become more aware of our eating behaviors and make healthier choices. Developing healthy coping strategies for managing emotions, such as mindfulness, exercise, or talking to a supportive person, can help reduce the reliance on food as a coping mechanism. It's also important to pay attention to our nutritional needs and make conscious choices about the foods we consume, considering their impact on both our physical and emotional well-being.

Emotional eating and its impact on health and well-being

Emotional eating, or using food as a way to cope with emotions, can have a significant impact on health and well-being. While it may provide temporary comfort or relief, emotional eating can have negative consequences on physical, emotional, and mental health.

Here are some ways emotional eating can impact health and well-being:

- **Weight gain and obesity**

Emotional eating often involves consuming high-calorie, high-sugar, or high-fat foods, which can lead to weight gain and obesity over time. Consuming excess calories can result in a positive energy balance, leading to weight gain and increased risk of various health issues, such as heart disease, diabetes, and certain cancers.

- **Poor nutrition**

Emotional eating tends to focus on comfort foods that are often low in essential nutrients and high in empty calories. This can lead to a poor overall nutritional intake, resulting in nutrient deficiencies and imbalances, which can negatively impact overall health and well-being.

- **Emotional and mental health issues**

Relying on food as a coping mechanism for emotions can perpetuate a cycle of emotional distress. Emotional eating may not address the underlying emotional issues and may even contribute to increased feelings of guilt, shame, or self-blame, leading to emotional and mental health issues such as depression, anxiety, and low self-esteem.

- **Loss of hunger and fullness cues**

Emotional eating can disrupt the body's natural hunger and fullness cues. Eating in response to emotions, rather than physiological hunger, can result in a loss of sensitivity to hunger and fullness signals, leading to overeating and difficulties in maintaining a healthy relationship with food.

- **Reduced ability to cope with emotions**

Relying solely on food as a coping mechanism for emotions can inhibit the development of healthy emotional coping strategies. It can prevent individuals from learning and practicing other effective ways of managing emotions, such as mindfulness, relaxation techniques, exercise, or seeking support from friends, family, or mental health professionals.

- **Impact on self-esteem and body image**

Emotional eating can contribute to negative self-esteem and body image issues. Weight gain or loss of control over eating can result in feelings of guilt, shame, and dissatisfaction with one's body, leading to further emotional distress and a negative impact on overall well-being.

It's important to recognize emotional eating patterns and develop healthy coping strategies for managing emotions. Seeking support from a therapist, counselor, or registered dietitian can be helpful in addressing emotional eating behaviors and developing healthier ways of managing emotions. Practicing mindful eating, engaging in regular physical activity, and finding alternative ways to cope with emotions, such as journaling, talking to a trusted friend, or engaging in relaxation techniques, can also be beneficial for improving overall health and well-being.

Strategies for managing emotional eating and developing healthier coping mechanisms

Managing emotional eating and developing healthier coping mechanisms can be a challenging process, but it's possible with effort and practice.

The following strategies can be helpful:

- **Awareness and mindfulness**

Developing awareness of emotional eating patterns is the first step in managing it. Pay attention to your emotions and the triggers that lead to emotional eating. Practice mindfulness by bringing non-judgmental awareness to your thoughts, feelings, and physical sensations when you have the urge to eat in response to emotions. Take a pause before reaching for food and ask yourself if you are truly hungry or if there is an emotional need that can be addressed in a healthier way.

- **Find alternative coping mechanisms**

Instead of turning to food, find alternative ways to cope with emotions. Engage in activities that you enjoy, such as hobbies, exercise, meditation, or spending time with loved ones. Find what works best for you by experimenting with different coping strategies. It may take some trial and error, but finding healthier ways to manage emotions can be empowering and beneficial for your overall well-being.

- **Practice self-care**

Taking care of yourself in non-food-related ways can help reduce emotional eating. Get enough sleep, manage stress through relaxation techniques, practice self-compassion, and prioritize self-care activities that bring you joy and fulfillment. When you take care of yourself holistically, you are less likely to turn to food as a way to comfort or cope with emotions.

- **Challenge negative thoughts and beliefs**

Emotional eating is often fueled by negative thoughts and beliefs about oneself or the situation. Challenge these negative thoughts and beliefs by practicing cognitive restructuring techniques. Positive and affirming statements should be used to replace negative self-talk. Surround yourself with supportive and positive influences, and practice self-compassion and self-love.

- **Build a healthy relationship with food**

Cultivate a healthy and balanced approach to food by practicing mindful eating. Eat when you are physically hungry, pay attention to hunger and fullness cues, and savor the flavors and textures of food without judgment. Avoid restrictive diets or labeling foods as "good" or "bad," as this can contribute to emotional eating. Seek guidance from a registered dietitian for personalized nutrition advice and support in building a healthy relationship with food.

- **Seek support**

It's important to remember that managing emotional eating is a journey, and it's okay to seek support from others. Consider working with a therapist, counselor, or registered dietitian who specializes in emotional eating and can provide guidance, support, and tools for managing emotions in a healthy way. Connecting with friends, family, or a support group can also provide emotional support and accountability in your journey towards healthier coping mechanisms.

- **Practice self-compassion**

Be kind and compassionate to yourself throughout this process. Remember that emotional eating is a common struggle for many people, and it's not something to be ashamed of. Be patient with yourself, celebrate small victories, and practice self-compassion when setbacks occur. You should treat yourself with the same compassion and understanding that you would offer to a friend.

Remember that developing healthier coping mechanisms takes time and effort. Be patient with yourself and celebrate your progress, no matter how little. With practice, you can learn to manage emotions without relying on food and cultivate a healthy relationship with both your emotions and food.

Chapter 3

Cognitive Factors in Eating

Cognitive factors play a significant role in our eating behaviors, including our food choices, portion sizes, and eating habits.

Here are some of the key cognitive factors that influence our eating:

- **Food preferences**

Our food preferences are shaped by a variety of cognitive factors, including our past experiences with food, cultural and societal influences, and individual tastes and preferences. We are more likely to choose foods that we find appealing and enjoyable, even if they are not the healthiest options.

- **Attention and distraction**

Our attentional focus can influence our eating behaviors. Distractions such as watching TV, using our phones, or engaging in other activities while eating can lead to mindless eating, where we consume more calories without paying attention to our hunger and fullness cues.

- **Food labels and packaging**

The way food is labeled and packaged can influence our perception of its healthfulness and affect our food choices. For example, foods labeled as "low-fat" or "organic" may be perceived as healthier and more desirable, even if they are not necessarily the best option.

- **Portion sizes**

Our cognitive biases can lead us to eat more than we need. Research has shown that we tend to eat more when served larger portions, even if we are not hungry.

- **Beliefs and attitudes**

Our beliefs and attitudes about food can shape our eating behaviors. For example, individuals who view certain foods as "bad" or "unhealthy" may be more likely to engage in restrictive eating or binge eating behaviors.

- **Self-control and willpower**

Our ability to exert self-control and resist temptation plays a significant role in our eating behaviors. Research has shown that individuals with higher levels of self-control are better able to resist the temptation to overeat and maintain a healthy weight.

- **Social influences**

Our social context can also influence our eating behaviors. Eating with others can lead us to consume more food than we would if eating alone, and social norms and pressures can influence our food choices and eating habits.

Understanding these cognitive factors can help us develop strategies for managing our eating behaviors. For example, practicing mindful eating and paying attention to our hunger and fullness cues can help us make more mindful food choices and avoid overeating. Learning to recognize and challenge negative beliefs and attitudes about food can also help us develop a healthier relationship with food.

The role of beliefs, attitudes, and expectations in food preferences

Beliefs, attitudes, and expectations play an important role in our food preferences.

Here are some of the ways in which these cognitive factors can influence the foods we choose to eat:

- **Taste expectations**

Our expectations about how a food will taste can influence our food preferences. For example, if we expect a food to be spicy or sweet, we may be more likely to enjoy it if it meets those expectations.

- **Health beliefs**

Our beliefs about the healthiness of certain foods can also influence our food choices. For example, individuals who believe that vegetables are healthy may be more likely to choose them over other less healthy options.

- **Social norms**

Our beliefs about what foods are appropriate or acceptable to eat in certain situations can also influence our food choices. For example, if we believe that it is rude to decline food that is offered to us, we may be more likely to eat even if we are not hungry.

- **Personal values**

Our personal values can also play a role in our food preferences. For example, individuals who value sustainability may be more likely to choose foods that are produced in an environmentally friendly way.

- **Emotions**

Our emotional state can influence our food preferences. For example, if we are feeling stressed or anxious, we may be more likely to choose comfort foods that provide a sense of familiarity and security.

- **Past experiences**

Our past experiences with food can shape our food preferences. For example, if we had a positive experience with a certain food in the past, we may be more likely to choose it again in the future.

Understanding the role of beliefs, attitudes, and expectations in our food preferences can help us make more mindful food choices. By recognizing how these cognitive factors influence our food choices, we can work to develop a healthier and more balanced relationship with food.

The influence of cognitive biases and heuristics on food choices

Cognitive biases and heuristics are mental shortcuts and patterns of thinking that can influence our food choices.

Here are some common cognitive biases and heuristics that can impact our eating behaviors:

- **Availability heuristic**

This heuristic involves making decisions based on readily available information. In the context of food choices, we may be more likely to choose foods that are easily accessible or familiar, even if they may not be the healthiest option. For example, reaching for a bag of chips because they are readily available and require minimal effort, rather than choosing a healthier snack like fruits or vegetables.

- **Anchoring bias**

This bias involves relying too heavily on the first piece of information encountered when making decisions. In the context of food choices, we may be influenced by the initial information we receive about a food's taste, portion size, or price, which can anchor our perceptions and ultimately influence our choices. For example, if we see a large portion size advertised as a meal deal, we may be more likely to choose it, even if it exceeds our actual hunger or nutritional needs.

- **Confirmation bias**

This bias involves seeking and interpreting information in a way that confirms our preexisting beliefs or expectations. In the context of food choices, we may seek out information that supports our existing food preferences or beliefs about what is healthy or enjoyable to eat, and ignore information that challenges those beliefs. This can reinforce our existing eating patterns, whether they are healthy or not.

- **Overconfidence bias**

This bias involves overestimating our own abilities or knowledge. In the context of food choices, we may overestimate our ability to accurately estimate portion sizes, caloric content, or the nutritional value of foods. This can lead to inaccurate perceptions about the healthiness of our food choices and impact our overall eating habits.

- **Sunk cost fallacy**

This fallacy involves considering past investments in decision-making rather than evaluating the current situation objectively. In the context of food choices, we may feel compelled to finish a large portion of food, even if we are no longer hungry because we have already paid for it or feel guilty about wasting food.

- **Social influence bias**

This bias involves being influenced by the behavior or opinions of others. In the context of food choices, we may be influenced by what our peers or family members are eating, or by social norms around portion sizes or food preferences. This can impact our food choices, leading us to eat more or choose less healthy options in social settings.

Awareness of these cognitive biases and heuristics can help us make more mindful and informed food choices. By recognizing how these biases and heuristics can influence our eating behaviors, we can strive to make more rational and health-conscious decisions about what and how much we eat.

Cognitive-behavioral techniques for improving eating habits and promoting healthy behaviors

Cognitive-behavioral techniques are often used in psychology to help individuals improve their eating habits and promote healthier behaviors.

Here are some common cognitive-behavioral techniques that can be applied to eating behaviors:

- **Cognitive restructuring**

This technique involves identifying and challenging negative or unhelpful thoughts and beliefs about food, eating, and body image. By recognizing and reframing distorted or irrational thoughts, individuals can develop more balanced and realistic beliefs about food and their own eating behaviors. This can help reduce emotional eating, decrease guilt or shame associated with food, and promote healthier eating habits.

- **Self-monitoring**

Keeping track of one's eating behaviors, such as recording food intake, portion sizes, hunger and fullness cues, and emotional triggers for eating, can increase awareness and help individuals make more conscious and mindful food choices. Self-monitoring can also provide valuable data for identifying patterns or triggers for overeating, emotional eating, or other unhealthy eating behaviors.

- **Goal setting**

Setting realistic and specific goals related to eating behaviors, such as increasing vegetable intake, reducing portion sizes, or eating mindfully, can provide motivation and direction for making healthier food choices. Goals should be SMART (Specific, Measurable, Achievable, Relevant, Time-bound) to increase their effectiveness.

- **Problem-solving**

Identifying and addressing barriers or challenges to healthy eating, such as time constraints, stress, or emotional triggers, can help individuals develop strategies for overcoming these obstacles. Problem-solving techniques involve brainstorming solutions, evaluating pros and cons, and implementing action plans to manage challenges and promote healthy eating habits.

- **Stimulus control**

Modifying the environment to make healthy eating choices easier and unhealthy choices more difficult can help individuals improve their eating habits. Examples of stimulus control techniques include keeping healthy foods visible and accessible, minimizing the presence of tempting or trigger foods, and establishing regular eating patterns or routines.

- **Relaxation and stress management**

Managing stress and emotions can help prevent emotional eating and promote healthier eating behaviors. Techniques such as deep breathing, meditation, or other relaxation techniques can help individuals reduce stress and emotional distress, which may be triggers for unhealthy eating behaviors.

- **Social support**

Engaging in social support networks, such as friends, family, or support groups, can provide encouragement, motivation, and accountability for improving eating habits. Social support can also provide a sense of community and belonging, which can help individuals sustain healthy eating behaviors over the long term.

- **Cognitive-behavioral therapy (CBT)**

"CBT" is a structured and evidence-based therapeutic approach that combines cognitive and behavioral techniques to promote positive changes in thoughts, feelings, and behaviors related to eating. "CBT" can be delivered by trained mental health professionals and may involve individual or group therapy sessions to address cognitive distortions, improve emotional regulation, and develop healthy coping strategies for managing eating behaviors.

These are just some examples of cognitive-behavioral techniques that can be applied to improve eating habits and promote healthy behaviors. Working with a qualified healthcare professional, such as a registered dietitian, nutritionist, or psychologist, can provide personalized guidance and support in applying these techniques to individual circumstances and needs.

Chapter 4

Social and Environmental Influences on Eating

Social and environmental factors can have a significant impact on our eating behaviors.

Here are some examples of social and environmental influences on eating:

- **Social norms**

Social norms refer to the unwritten rules and expectations that guide behavior in a particular social context. These norms can influence what, when, and how much we eat. For example, if everyone at a party is eating unhealthy snacks, it may be difficult to resist the temptation to indulge. On the other hand, if eating healthy is the norm in a particular social circle, it may be easier to make healthy choices.

- **Cultural influences**

Cultural factors such as ethnicity, religion, and traditions can impact food choices and eating habits. Certain foods may be considered taboo or sacred, and cultural celebrations often involve specific foods. For example, in some cultures, it may be customary to eat large, heavy meals as a sign of hospitality or celebration, while in others, light and healthy meals may be preferred.

- **Food availability and accessibility**

The availability and accessibility of food in our environment can influence our eating behaviors. For example, if healthy food options are limited or expensive in a particular neighborhood, it may be more difficult to make healthy choices. Alternatively, if unhealthy foods are readily available and promoted in our environment, it may be harder to resist temptation and make healthy choices.

- **Food marketing and advertising**

Food marketing and advertising can influence our perceptions of what is healthy or desirable, and can impact our food choices. For example, advertising campaigns may promote unhealthy foods as "fun" or "indulgent," while healthier options may be portrayed as "boring" or "unappealing." Marketing techniques, such as packaging design and product placement, can also influence our purchasing decisions.

- **Social support and accountability**

Having social support and accountability can help reinforce healthy eating behaviors. For example, having a friend or partner who shares your goals for healthy eating can provide encouragement and motivation. Alternatively, joining a support group or working with a health coach or nutritionist can provide accountability and guidance for making healthy choices.

- **Food policies and regulations**

Government policies and regulations related to food, such as food labeling laws, can impact our food choices and eating behaviors. For example, clearer and more accurate food labels can help consumers make more informed decisions about the nutritional value of the food they consume.

Understanding the social and environmental factors that influence our eating behaviors can help us make more conscious and intentional choices about what and how we eat. By making small changes to our environment and building a support system, we can create a more supportive and healthy environment for our eating habits.

The impact of social norms and peer pressure on eating behavior

Social norms and peer pressure can have a significant impact on our eating behaviors. When we are in social situations, we often conform to the norms and expectations of the group. This can lead us to eat more or less than we normally would or to choose foods that we may not otherwise choose.

Here are some ways that social norms and peer pressure can influence eating behavior:

- **Portion sizes**

When eating in a group, we may be influenced by the portion sizes that others are eating. If everyone is eating large portions, we may feel pressure to do the same, even if it goes against our usual eating habits.

- **Food choices**

In social situations, we may be influenced by what others are eating. If everyone is eating unhealthy foods, we may feel pressure to do the same in order to fit in. Alternatively, if everyone is eating healthy foods, we may feel motivated to make healthier choices as well.

- **Eating speed**

When eating in a group, we may feel pressure to eat quickly in order to keep up with the pace of the meal. This can lead us to overeat, as we may not give ourselves enough time to feel full.

- **Snacking habits**

Social situations, such as parties or gatherings, may involve a lot of snacking. If others are snacking frequently, we may feel pressure to do the same, even if we are not hungry.

- **Peer influence**

Peer pressure can also play a role in eating behavior. If we are eating with friends who are pressuring us to eat more or less than we want to, it can be difficult to resist their influence.

It's important to be aware of the influence that social norms and peer pressure can have on our eating behavior. By being mindful of these influences and making conscious choices about what and how we eat, we can maintain a healthy relationship with food and avoid overeating or undereating in social situations. Additionally, by setting a positive example and encouraging healthy habits in our social circle, we can help create a supportive and healthy environment for everyone.

The role of food availability, accessibility, and convenience in shaping our choices

The availability, accessibility, and convenience of food can significantly shape our eating choices. These factors influence what foods are easily accessible to us, how convenient they are to obtain and consume, and ultimately, what we choose to eat.

Here are some key points on the role of food availability, accessibility, and convenience in shaping our choices:

- **Food availability**

The availability of different types of food in our environment can greatly impact our choices. If unhealthy, highly processed foods are readily available and visible in our surroundings, we may be more likely to choose and consume them. On the other hand, if healthy foods such as fruits and vegetables are easily accessible and visible, we may be more inclined to choose them.

- **Food accessibility**

Accessibility refers to how easily we can obtain and reach different types of food. Foods that are highly accessible, such as those that are within arm's reach or at eye level in our home or workplace, are more likely to be consumed frequently. For example, having a bowl of fruit on the counter or keeping healthy snacks at eye level in the pantry can make them more accessible and increase the likelihood of choosing them.

- **Convenience**

Convenience plays a significant role in our food choices. In today's fast-paced world, we often prioritize convenience in our food decisions. Foods that are quick and easy to prepare, or that are available as pre-packaged or fast-food options, are often chosen for their convenience, even if they may not be the healthiest options. On the other hand, healthy foods that require more time and effort to prepare may be less likely to be chosen due to their perceived inconvenience.

- **Food marketing and advertising**

Food marketing and advertising also play a role in shaping our choices. The marketing and advertising of certain foods can create a perception of convenience, affordability, and desirability, influencing our food choices. For example, the promotion of fast food or sugary beverages as quick and convenient options can influence our decision-making, even if they are not the healthiest choices.

- **Food environment**

The overall food environment, including the availability of grocery stores, farmers' markets, and restaurants in our neighborhood, can impact our food choices. If healthy food options are not easily accessible in our environment, it can be challenging to make healthy choices.

Understanding the influence of food availability, accessibility, and convenience on our food choices is crucial in developing healthy eating habits. By making healthy foods more available, accessible, and convenient in our environment, we can shape our choices towards more nutritious options. Additionally, being mindful of the marketing and advertising tactics used by the food industry can help us make informed choices and prioritize our health and well-being.

Strategies for navigating social and environmental factors to make healthier food choices

Navigating social and environmental factors to make healthier food choices may require some conscious effort and planning.

The following strategies can be helpful:

- **Create a healthy food environment**

Make healthy foods readily available and accessible in your environment. Keep a variety of fresh fruits and vegetables, whole grains, lean proteins, and other nutritious options stocked in your pantry, refrigerator, and workplace. Make unhealthy options less visible and less convenient, and keep them out of reach, if possible.

- **Plan and prepare meals ahead of time**

Planning and preparing meals in advance can help you make healthier choices. Set aside time for meal planning and grocery shopping, and prepare meals in bulk to have healthy options available throughout the week. This can reduce the temptation to choose less healthy options when you're hungry and pressed for time.

- **Practice mindful eating**

Pay attention to your hunger and fullness cues, and listen to your body's signals. Don't eat when you're stressed, bored, or under social pressure. Eat slowly and savor each bite, and try to eat without distractions, such as TV or screens, to be more mindful of your food choices and portion sizes.

- **Seek support from others**

Surround yourself with supportive individuals who share your health goals. Engage in social activities that don't revolve solely around food, such as going for a walk or doing a group exercise class. Having a support system can help you stay accountable and motivated to make healthier food choices.

- **Practice assertiveness**

Learn to say "no" politely when faced with social pressure to eat unhealthy foods. You can explain that you are trying to make healthier choices for your well-being or offer an alternative, such as suggesting a healthier option or bringing your own dish to gatherings.

- **Educate yourself about food marketing and advertising**

Be aware of the tactics used by the food industry to promote less healthy foods, such as exaggerated health claims, attractive packaging, and celebrity endorsements. Educate yourself about nutrition and food labels, and make informed choices based on the actual nutritional content of foods, rather than marketing messages.

- **Seek professional guidance**

Consider consulting with a registered dietitian or nutritionist for personalized guidance on making healthier food choices. They can provide tailored advice and strategies to help you navigate social and environmental factors that may influence your food choices.

Remember that making healthier food choices is a lifelong journey, and it's important to be patient and kind to yourself. Small, sustainable changes over time can lead to long-term success in developing healthier eating habits.

Chapter 5

Eating Disorders and Disordered Eating

Eating disorders and disordered eating are serious mental health conditions that can have significant physical and emotional consequences. These conditions involve abnormal eating behaviors that can lead to malnutrition, dehydration, and other health problems. Eating disorders are diagnosed when these behaviors meet specific criteria outlined in the **Diagnostic and Statistical Manual of Mental Disorders (DSM-5),** while disordered eating refers to a range of abnormal eating behaviors that may not meet the criteria for a specific diagnosis.

Common types of eating disorders include:

- **Anorexia nervosa**

Intense fear of gaining weight and body image distortion are what characterized anorexia nervosa.

People with anorexia often severely restrict their food intake and may engage in other behaviors, such as excessive exercise, to lose weight.

- **Bulimia nervosa**

Bulimia nervosa involves a cycle of binge eating followed by purging behaviors, such as self-induced vomiting or laxative use, to try to rid the body of the calories consumed during the binge.

- **Binge-eating disorder**

Binge-eating disorder is characterized by recurrent episodes of binge eating, during which a person consumes a large amount of food in a short period of time and feels a sensation of being unable to control their eating.

- **Avoidant/restrictive food intake disorder (ARFID)**

"ARFID" involves a persistent lack of interest in food or a limited range of food intake, often resulting in significant weight loss and nutritional deficiencies.

- **Other specified feeding or eating disorder (OSFED)**

"OSFED" includes a range of eating disorder behaviors that do not meet the criteria for a specific diagnosis.

Disordered eating may involve any number of abnormal eating behaviors, such as restrictive eating, binge eating, purging, or compulsive exercise. These behaviors can lead to physical and emotional consequences similar to those experienced by individuals with diagnosed eating disorders.

Treatment for eating disorders and disordered eating typically involves a combination of psychological therapy, nutritional counseling, and medical treatment, depending on the severity of the condition. Early intervention is important to prevent the development of long-term health problems and to improve the chances of recovery.

An overview of the diagnostic criteria for eating disorders

Here's an overview of the diagnostic criteria for some of the most common eating disorders as outlined in the **Diagnostic and Statistical Manual of Mental Disorders, 5th Edition (DSM-5),** which is a commonly used reference for mental health professionals:

Anorexia nervosa:

- Restriction of energy intake leading to substantially low body weight for age, sex, developmental trajectory, and physical health.
- Intense fear about putting on weight or becoming fat, or persistently engaging in behaviors that prevent weight gain even though at a considerably low weight.
- A disturbance in how one experiences their body weight or shape, undue influence of body weight or shape on self-evaluation, or a denial of the seriousness of the current low body weight.

Bulimia nervosa:

- Recurrent episodes of binge eating are characterized by eating an unusually large amount of food within a discrete period of time and a sense of lack of control over eating during the episode.
- Recurrent improper compensatory behaviors to avoid weight gain, such as self-induced vomiting, abuse of laxatives, diuretics, or other drugs, fasting, or excessive exercise.
- The binge eating and improper compensatory behaviors both occur, on average, at least once per week for three months.
- Weight and body shape unduly influenced self-evaluation.

Binge eating disorder:

- Recurrent episodes of binge eating are characterized by eating an unusually large amount of food within a discrete period of time and a sense of lack of control over eating during the episode.

- Binge eating episodes are associated with three or more of the following: *eating much more rapidly than normal, eating until uncomfortably full, eating large amounts of food when not physically hungry, eating alone due to embarrassment, feeling disgusted with oneself, depressed, or guilty after binge eating.*
- Marked distress regarding binge eating.
- Over the course of three months, binge eating occurs on average at least once every week.

It's important to note that these are brief summaries and the full diagnostic criteria for eating disorders are more detailed and nuanced. Accurate diagnosis and treatment should be done by qualified mental health professionals, and early intervention is crucial for better outcomes. If you suspect that you or someone you know may have an eating disorder, it's important to seek professional help for a comprehensive evaluation and appropriate treatment.

The prevalence and consequences of disordered eating behaviors

Disordered eating behaviors are quite common and can have significant physical and psychological consequences. According to the **National Eating Disorders Association (NEDA),** the prevalence of disordered eating behaviors is estimated to be as high as 10% of the general population.

The following are some of the consequences that can result from disordered eating behaviors:

- **Physical health consequences**

Disordered eating behaviors can result in a variety of physical health problems, including malnutrition, gastrointestinal problems, cardiovascular disease, electrolyte imbalances, and other medical complications.

- **Psychological consequences**

Disordered eating behaviors can have a significant impact on mental health, including depression, anxiety, low self-esteem, and impaired cognitive function. In severe cases, eating disorders can lead to suicidal ideation and suicide attempts.

- **Social consequences**

Disordered eating behaviors can interfere with relationships and social activities, leading to isolation and loneliness.

- **Occupational consequences**

Disordered eating behaviors can affect work and academic performance, leading to absenteeism, decreased productivity, and impaired cognitive function.

It's important to note that disordered eating behaviors can range from mild to severe and that not all individuals who engage in disordered eating behaviors meet the diagnostic criteria for an eating disorder. Nevertheless, disordered eating behaviors can still have significant physical and psychological consequences, and it's important to seek help if you or someone you know is struggling with these issues.

Evidence-based treatments for eating disorders and related conditions

Several evidence-based treatments have been developed for eating disorders and related conditions.

Below are some of the most commonly used treatments:

- **Cognitive Behavioral Therapy (CBT)**

"CBT" is a type of talk therapy that has been shown to be effective in the treatment of eating disorders. The goal of "CBT" is to help individuals identify and change negative thought patterns and behaviors that contribute to disordered eating.

- **Family-Based Therapy (FBT)**

"FBT" is a type of therapy that involves the family in the treatment of adolescent eating disorders. The goal of "FBT" is to help parents take an active role in their child's recovery and to support the adolescent in restoring healthy eating habits.

- **Interpersonal Psychotherapy (IPT)**

"IPT" is a type of talk therapy that focuses on improving interpersonal relationships and communication skills. "IPT" has been shown to be effective in the treatment of bulimia nervosa and binge eating disorder.

- **Dialectical Behavior Therapy (DBT)**

"DBT" is a type of talk therapy that combines cognitive-behavioral techniques with mindfulness practices. When treating binge eating disorder, "DBT" has been shown to be effective.

- **Medication**

Antidepressants and other medications have been used to treat eating disorders, particularly bulimia nervosa and binge eating disorder. However, medication should be used in conjunction with therapy and under the guidance of a physician.

It's important to note that treatment should be tailored to the individual's needs and that a multidisciplinary approach is often necessary for successful treatment of eating disorders. This may include medical monitoring, nutritional counseling, and support groups. Early intervention is also crucial in the treatment of eating disorders, as the longer an individual goes without treatment, the more difficult it may be to recover.

Chapter 6

Mindful Eating and Intuitive Eating

Mindful eating and intuitive eating are two approaches to eating that focus on developing a healthy relationship with food, promoting self-awareness, and cultivating a positive mindset towards eating. These approaches are not strict diets, but rather mindful and intuitive ways of eating that prioritize listening to one's body and honoring its natural cues.

Mindful Eating

Mindful eating involves paying full attention to the experience of eating, being present in the moment, and engaging all the senses to fully appreciate the food. It involves eating slowly, savoring each bite, and being aware of hunger and fullness cues. Mindful eating also encourages non-judgmental awareness of thoughts, emotions, and cravings that may arise during eating, without engaging in impulsive or emotional eating.

Intuitive Eating

Intuitive eating is a philosophy that encourages individuals to trust their own internal cues of hunger, fullness, and satisfaction. It involves listening to the body's hunger signals, eating when hungry, and stopping when full. Intuitive eating also emphasizes giving oneself permission to eat all foods without guilt or shame and promoting a healthy relationship with food and body image.

Both mindful eating and intuitive eating have been shown to have several potential benefits, including:

- **Improved eating behaviors**

Both approaches can help individuals develop a healthier relationship with food, reduce emotional eating, and improve awareness of hunger and fullness cues.

- **Enhanced body awareness**

Mindful eating and intuitive eating promote increased self-awareness and body acceptance, which can lead to a healthier body image and improved self-esteem.

- **Weight management**

Research suggests that mindful eating and intuitive eating may be associated with healthier weight management, as they promote a balanced and sustainable approach to eating that is not focused on strict diets or restrictions.

- **Improved mental health**

Both approaches can also have positive impacts on mental health, as they encourage self-compassion, reduce guilt and shame associated with eating, and promote a positive mindset towards food and the body.

It's important to note that mindful eating and intuitive eating may not be suitable for everyone, and individualized guidance from a qualified healthcare professional or registered dietitian may be necessary for those with specific health concerns or conditions.

The principles and benefits of mindful and intuitive eating

Here is an expanded version of the principles and benefits of mindful and intuitive eating:

Principles of Mindful Eating

• Paying attention

Mindful eating involves fully focusing on the experience of eating, without distractions. It involves being present in the moment and fully engaging the senses to appreciate the flavors, textures, and smells of food.

• Eating slowly

Mindful eating encourages eating slowly and savoring each bite, allowing time for the body to register its hunger and fullness cues.

• Listening to hunger and fullness cues

Mindful eating emphasizes tuning into the body's signals of hunger and fullness, and eating in response to these cues rather than external cues such as portion sizes or social norms.

- **Non-judgmental awareness**

Mindful eating encourages a non-judgmental awareness of thoughts, emotions, and cravings that may arise during eating, without engaging in impulsive or emotional eating.

- **Cultivating gratitude**

Mindful eating involves developing a sense of gratitude towards the food we eat and appreciating the effort that goes into producing it.

Principles of Intuitive Eating

- **Trusting internal cues**

Intuitive eating encourages individuals to trust their body's natural cues of hunger, fullness, and satisfaction, and to eat in response to these cues.

- **Rejecting diet mentality**

Intuitive eating promotes letting go of dieting and restrictive eating patterns, and embracing a healthy and balanced approach to eating that is not focused on weight or appearance.

- **Emphasizing body acceptance**

Intuitive eating promotes body acceptance and self-compassion, regardless of size, shape, or weight.

- **Coping with emotions without food**

Intuitive eating encourages finding alternative ways to cope with emotions other than using food, such as developing healthy coping mechanisms and addressing emotional needs directly.

- **Honoring food preferences**

Intuitive eating allows individuals to enjoy all foods without guilt or shame, and encourages listening to food preferences and cravings without judgment.

Benefits of Mindful and Intuitive Eating

- **Improved eating behaviors**

Both mindful eating and intuitive eating can help individuals develop a healthier relationship with food, reduce emotional eating, and improve awareness of hunger and fullness cues.

- **Enhanced body awareness**

Mindful eating and intuitive eating promote increased self-awareness and body acceptance, which can lead to a healthier body image and improved self-esteem.

- **Weight management**

Research suggests that mindful eating and intuitive eating may be associated with healthier weight management, as they promote a balanced and sustainable approach to eating that is not focused on strict diets or restrictions.

- **Improved mental health**

Both approaches can have positive impacts on mental health, as they encourage self-compassion, reduce guilt and shame associated with eating, and promote a positive mindset towards food and the body.

- **Enhanced overall well-being**

Mindful and intuitive eating can promote a healthy relationship with food, improve body satisfaction, and enhance overall well-being, leading to a better quality of life.

It's important to note that mindful and intuitive eating may not be suitable for everyone, and individualized guidance from a qualified healthcare professional or registered dietitian may be necessary for those with specific health concerns or conditions.

Techniques for cultivating mindfulness and intuition in eating

Here are some techniques for cultivating mindfulness and intuition in eating:

- **Slow down**

Eating slowly allows you to fully experience the taste, texture, and aroma of food, and helps you tune in to your body's hunger and fullness cues. Take small bites, chew thoroughly, and savor each mouthful.

- **Eliminate distractions**

Minimize distractions during meals by turning off screens, putting away your phone, and focusing solely on your meal. Pay attention to the smells, colors, and flavors of the food.

- **Engage your senses**

Use your senses to fully experience your food. Notice the colors, shapes, smells, tastes, and textures of the food. Appreciate the sensory experience of eating without judgment.

- **Check-in with hunger and fullness cues**

Before eating, check in with your body to assess your hunger level. During the meal, periodically pause and assess your fullness level. Eat until you feel comfortably full, and avoid overeating.

- **Cultivate non-judgmental awareness**

Practice observing your thoughts, emotions, and cravings without judgment during meals. Notice any thoughts or emotions that arise without reacting to them. Be compassionate towards yourself and your eating experience.

- **Practice mindful food selection**

Take the time to choose foods that truly satisfy you and align with your body's needs, rather than eating based on external cues or emotional triggers. Consider the nutritional value and how the food makes you feel.

- **Listen to your body**

Cultivate a deeper connection with your body and listen to its signals. Trust your body's wisdom and eat in response to its cues rather than external rules or societal norms.

- **Develop healthy coping mechanisms**

Instead of using food as a coping mechanism for emotions, develop healthy coping strategies such as exercise, meditation, journaling, talking to a friend, or engaging in a hobby.

- **Practice self-compassion**

Be kind and compassionate towards yourself in your eating journey. Avoid self-criticism or guilt over food choices, and instead practice self-compassion and forgiveness.

- **Seek support**

If you find it challenging to cultivate mindfulness and intuition in eating on your own, consider seeking support from a registered dietitian, therapist, or other healthcare professional who can provide guidance and assistance.

Remember, developing mindful and intuitive eating habits takes time and practice. Be patient with yourself and approach it with a non-judgmental attitude. Every small step towards mindfulness and intuition in eating can make a positive impact on your relationship with food and overall well-being.

The role of mindfulness and intuition in promoting sustainable, healthy eating habits

Mindfulness and intuition can play a significant role in promoting sustainable, healthy eating habits.

Here are some ways in which mindfulness and intuition can contribute to healthy eating:

- **Increased awareness of hunger and fullness cues**

Mindfulness helps you become more attuned to your body's hunger and fullness cues. By paying close attention to your body's signals, you can eat in response to physical hunger and stop eating when you feel comfortably full, which can prevent overeating and promote healthy portion sizes.

- **Improved food choices**

Mindfulness allows you to become more aware of the nutritional value and quality of the foods you choose to eat. It can help you make more informed decisions about what foods truly satisfy you and align with your body's needs, rather than making impulsive or emotional food choices.

- **Reduced emotional eating**

Mindfulness helps you develop a greater understanding of your emotions and the triggers for emotional eating. By being present and non-judgmental towards your emotions, you can learn to respond to them in healthier ways, such as through self-care or seeking support, rather than turning to food for comfort.

- **Enhanced taste and enjoyment of food**

Mindfulness allows you to fully experience the taste, texture, and aroma of food, which can enhance your enjoyment of eating. This can lead to a more satisfying and pleasurable eating experience, and reduce the tendency to eat mindlessly or emotionally.

- **Greater connection with your body**

Mindfulness encourages a deeper connection with your body, helping you tune into its needs and signals. This can help you become more attuned to your body's hunger and fullness cues, cravings, and other physiological sensations, allowing you to respond to them in a healthy and intuitive manner.

- **Reduced reliance on external cues**

Mindfulness encourages you to rely less on external cues, such as societal norms, portion sizes, or external rules, and instead tune into your inner wisdom and intuition when making food choices. This can help you develop a more sustainable and flexible eating pattern that is aligned with your unique needs and preferences.

- **Development of healthy coping mechanisms**

Mindfulness helps you develop healthier coping mechanisms for dealing with stress, emotions, and other triggers, rather than turning to food as a primary coping strategy. This can promote emotional resilience and reduce the reliance on food for emotional regulation.

Overall, mindfulness and intuition can help foster a more sustainable, healthy, and balanced relationship with food. By developing a deeper awareness and connection with your body, emotions, and food choices, you can make more informed decisions, eat in response to your body's needs, and develop healthier coping mechanisms for managing emotions and stress.

Conclusion

Applying Psychology to Your Eating Habits

In conclusion, understanding the psychology of eating can provide valuable insights into how our minds influence our food choices and eating behaviors. By examining the biological, cognitive, emotional, social, and environmental factors that shape our eating habits, we can develop a deeper understanding of our relationship with food and make positive changes for our health and well-being.

Throughout this book, we explored various topics related to the psychology of eating, including the role of psychology in shaping our eating habits, the influence of culture, media, and advertising on our food choices, the importance of mindfulness and self-awareness in eating, the biology of appetite and satiety, emotions and eating, cognitive factors in eating, social and environmental influences on eating, as well as eating disorders and disordered eating.

We also discussed evidence-based strategies and techniques for managing emotional eating, improving eating habits, promoting mindful and intuitive eating, and developing healthy coping mechanisms. By applying the principles of psychology to our eating habits, we can make more informed, mindful, and intuitive food choices that align with our body's needs, preferences, and overall well-being.

In today's fast-paced world with an abundance of food options, it's crucial to develop a healthy and balanced relationship with food. By understanding the psychological factors that influence our eating behaviors, we can make empowered choices and develop sustainable, healthy eating habits that promote our physical, mental, and emotional health.

Remember, changing eating habits takes time and effort, and it's important to approach it with self-compassion and patience. By incorporating the knowledge and strategies discussed in this book into your daily life, you can develop a healthier and more fulfilling relationship with food, and ultimately improve your overall health and well-being.

Key takeaways and actionable tips for improving your eating habits

Here are some key takeaways and actionable tips for improving your eating habits:

- Pay close attention to your body's hunger and satiety cues. Eat when you are hungry, and stop eating when you feel comfortably satisfied.
- Practice mindfulness and intuition in eating. Focus on the experience of eating, savor your food, and listen to your body's cues.
- Include whole grains, fruits, vegetables, lean proteins, and healthy fats in your diet as well as a variety of other nutrient-dense foods.
- Avoid strict diets or restrictive eating patterns, as they can lead to disordered eating behaviors and nutrient deficiencies.
- Be aware of the social and environmental factors that influence your food choices. Surround yourself with supportive people

and make healthy food choices easily accessible.

- Address emotional eating by developing healthy coping mechanisms, such as exercise, meditation, or talking to a therapist.
- Seek professional help if you are struggling with disordered eating behaviors or an eating disorder. Evidence-based treatments, such as cognitive-behavioral therapy, can help you develop a healthier relationship with food and your body.

Remember that improving your eating habits is a process that takes time and effort. Start by incorporating small, sustainable changes into your daily routine, and celebrate your progress along the way. With self-awareness, mindfulness, and self-compassion, you can develop a healthy and balanced relationship with food that supports your overall health and well-being.

The benefits of incorporating psychological principles into your approach to food and nutrition

Incorporating psychological principles into your approach to food and nutrition can have numerous benefits, including:

- **Improved eating habits**

Understanding the psychological factors that influence your food choices, such as emotions, beliefs, and social influences, can help you make more informed and intentional decisions about what, when, and how much you eat. This can lead to improved eating habits, such as choosing nutrient-dense foods, eating mindfully, and listening to your body's hunger and fullness cues.

- **Better management of emotional eating**

Emotional eating can be a common challenge for many people, but by gaining insight into the emotional triggers behind your eating behaviors, you can develop healthier coping mechanisms and reduce emotional eating. This can lead to improved emotional well-being and overall health.

- **Increased self-awareness**

Paying attention to your thoughts, feelings, and behaviors related to food and nutrition can increase your self-awareness. This self-awareness can help you identify patterns, habits, and triggers that may be contributing to unhealthy eating behaviors, and empower you to make positive changes.

- **Enhanced relationship with food and body**

Developing a healthy and balanced relationship with food and your body is crucial for overall well-being. By understanding the psychological factors that influence your relationship with food, such as body image, self-esteem, and cognitive biases, you can cultivate a positive and compassionate relationship with food and your body.

- **Sustainable and long-term changes**

Incorporating psychological principles into your approach to food and nutrition can help you develop sustainable and long-term changes in your eating habits. Rather than relying on short-term diets or restrictive eating patterns, understanding the psychological factors at play can help you make lasting changes that support your overall health and well-being.

- **Enhanced overall health**

Improved eating habits and a healthy relationship with food can have a positive impact on your physical health. Eating a balanced diet that meets your body's nutrient needs can support optimal physical health, energy levels, and disease prevention.

- **Increased enjoyment of food**

Eating mindfully, being aware of your senses, and savoring your food can enhance your enjoyment of the eating experience. By incorporating psychological principles into your approach to food and nutrition, you can cultivate a positive and enjoyable relationship with food, which can enhance your overall well-being.

In summary, incorporating psychological principles into your approach to food and nutrition can have numerous benefits, including improved eating habits, better management of emotional eating, increased self-awareness, enhanced relationship with food and body, sustainable and long-term changes, enhanced overall health, and increased enjoyment of food. Understanding the psychological factors that influence your eating behaviors can empower you to make informed choices and develop a healthy and balanced relationship with food that supports your overall well-being.

The potential for continued growth and learning in the pursuit of healthy eating habits

The pursuit of healthy eating habits is a lifelong journey that involves continuous growth and learning. As you gain insights into the psychological factors that influence your eating behaviors and develop strategies to improve your relationship with food, you can continue to evolve and make positive changes in your eating habits.

Here are some tips for continued growth and learning in the pursuit of healthy eating habits:

- **Stay curious and open-minded**

Approach your journey towards healthy eating habits with curiosity and an open mind. Be willing to explore and learn about different psychological factors that may impact your eating behaviors, such as emotions, beliefs, attitudes, and social influences. Stay open to trying new strategies and approaches that align with your goals and values.

- **Reflect and evaluate**

Regularly reflect on your eating habits, emotions, and thoughts related to food. Evaluate what is working well for you and what areas may need improvement. This reflection can help you gain insights into your patterns and behaviors, and guide you in making adjustments to support healthier eating habits.

- **Set realistic and flexible goals**

Set realistic and flexible goals that are aligned with your individual needs, preferences, and lifestyle. Avoid rigid or extreme dieting approaches, as they can be unsustainable and counterproductive. Instead, focus on setting achievable and adaptable goals that promote a balanced and nourishing relationship with food.

- **Seek support**

Surround yourself with a supportive environment that encourages healthy eating habits. This can include seeking support from loved ones, friends, or health professionals, such as registered dietitians or psychologists, who can provide guidance and assistance in developing healthy eating behaviors.

- **Practice self-compassion**

Be kind and compassionate towards yourself as you navigate your journey towards healthy eating habits. Avoid self-judgment or self-blame for any setbacks or challenges you may encounter. Instead, practice self-compassion and forgiveness, and view setbacks as opportunities for learning and growth.

- **Stay mindful and intuitive**

Incorporate mindfulness and intuition into your eating practices. Practice mindful eating by paying attention to your senses, eating slowly, and savoring your food. Listen to your body's hunger and fullness cues, and trust your intuition when it comes to making food choices that nourish your body and support your overall well-being.

- **Continuously educate yourself**

Stay informed and continuously educate yourself about nutrition, psychology, and other relevant topics related to healthy eating habits. Stay up-to-date with reliable sources of information, research, and evidence-based guidelines, and be willing to adapt your knowledge and strategies as new information emerges.

Remember, healthy eating habits are not about perfection, but rather about progress and continuous improvement. Embrace the journey of growth and learning, and be patient with yourself as you develop a healthy and balanced relationship with food. With time, effort, and self-compassion, you can continue to evolve and thrive in your pursuit of healthy eating habits.

Printed in Dunstable, United Kingdom

65077679R00067